FU

Ex

A journal so you can destroy,
rant and vent without receiving
a restraining order

By Alex A. Lluch

WS Publishing Group
San Diego, California 92119

FU EX:
A journal so you can destroy, rant and vent
without receiving a restraining order

By Alex A. Lluch
Published by WS Publishing Group
San Diego, California 92119
© Copyright 2010 by WS Publishing Group

WS Publishing Group makes no claims whatsoever regarding the interpretation
or utilization of any information contained herein and/or recorded by the user
of this book. If you utilize any information provided in this book, you do so at
your own risk and you specifically waive any right to make any claim against the
author and publisher, its officers, directors, employees or representatives as the
result of the use of such information.

Design by:
David Defenbaugh, Sarah Jang; WS Publishing Group

Image credits:
drunk guy, pg.77 © iStockphoto/Shannon Toth

For more information on this and many other best-selling books visit
www.WSPublishingGroup.com.
E-mail: info@WSPublishingGroup.com

ISBN 13: 978-1-934386-96-5

Printed in China

Write a WARNING

on this page to anyone
who finds this book.

de•file
verb

1 a: to corrupt the purity or perfection of
<I will feel better after I defile this journal>

abuse • besmirch • dirty • pollute • sully • tarnish

Tape a photo of your ex here.

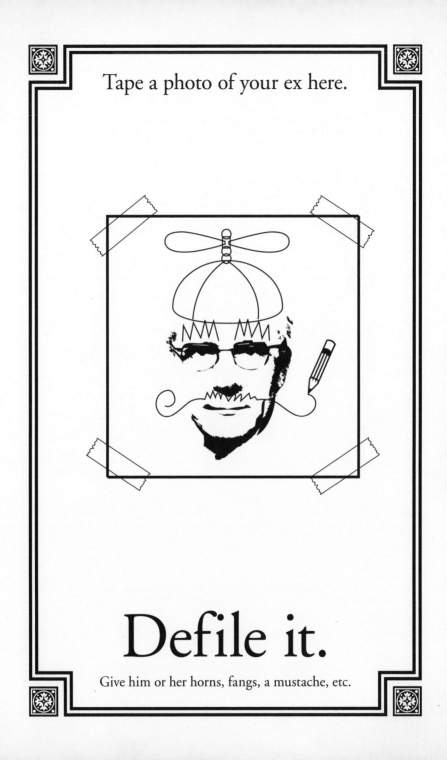

Defile it.

Give him or her horns, fangs, a mustache, etc.

tag
verb

1: to deface with graffiti
<I would love to tag your precious vehicle>

brand • deface • mark up • sully • desecrate

TAG your ex's car.

Write all the mean
names you'd love
to call your ex to
his or her face.

col•lage
noun

1: a creative work that resembles such a composition in incorporating various materials or elements
<I enjoyed making a collage out of your face>

hodgepodge • patchwork • smattering • mishmosh

Make a **COLLAGE**

out of a photo of the two of you.

Tear the photo into little pieces and
glue them here haphazardly.

gross
adjective

2: inspiring disgust or distaste
<The sound of your name is so gross>

unrefined • tasteless • ugly • disgusting • lewd

You **Gross** Me Out!

Rearrange the letters of your ex's name
to make gross-sounding words.

spell
noun

1 a: spoken word or form of words
held to have magic power
<I am working on a spell that will
turn my ex into a pig>

bewitchment • charm • enchantment • incantation

Cast a SPELL

Choose the misfortune that will befall your ex.

INSTRUCTIONS:

- Clip a lock of your hair and place it in a bowl

- Pour in ½ cup of vinegar

- Add 2 pinches of salt

- Stir counterclockwise

- Chant your ex's name 6 times

Now, check off which effect you want the spell to have on your ex.

☐ Have toes as fingers

☐ Grow excessive body hair

☐ Smell like raw onions

☐ Make all foods taste like dirt

☐ Inexplicable fear of cute baby animals

stomp
verb

1: to step heavily so as to bruise, crush, or injure
<My ex likes to stomp on my dreams >

trample • smash • squash • pound • crush • scuff

STOMP

Think of all the times your
ex walked all over you.
Now stomp on this page
with your dirty shoe.

poke
verb

1 a: to prod or pierce with or as if with a sharp object
<I will poke this voodoo doll until I feel better>

jab • prod • push • stab • thrust • assail

Pretend this voodoo doll is your ex. Poke it with a sharp object.

poke

poke

poke

poke

poke

poke

poke

poke

poke

poke

scathing
adjective

1: bitterly critical remarks
<I wish I could send you this scathing letter>

brutal • biting • cutting • harsh • blunt • nasty

Write a
SCATHING LETTER
to your ex

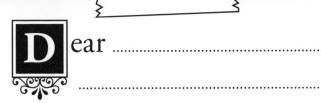

Dear ....

....

....

....

....

....

....

....

....

....

....

The
Nightmare
Ex

mov•ie
noun

1: a motion picture
<A movie about our relationship would be a horror film>

film • cinema • flick • picture show • video

They're making a MOVIE
about you and your ex's relationship.

Fill out the director's notes below.

Movie title: ....

Starring .... as you.

Starring .... as your ex.

Supporting cast: ....

....

....

Summary: ....

....

....

....

....

....

....

This film is rated R for: ....

VS.

gen•der
noun

1 b: the behavioral, cultural, or psychological traits typically associated with one sex
<I can't figure out what the F*&$ is wrong with the opposite gender>

gal • guy • girl • boy • woman • man • female • male

Make a list of things you
hate about the other **gender**.

heart
noun

1: one's innermost emotions, inclinations, or affection
<Thanks for crushing my heart>

love • emotions • affection • sentiment • feelings

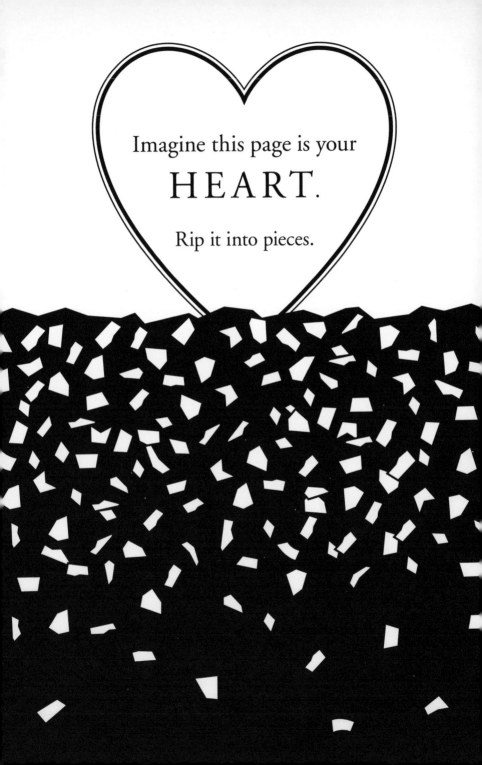

Imagine this page is your

HEART.

Rip it into pieces.

crap•py
adjective

1: inferior in quality, lousy
<My ex's friends are all crappy by association>

crummy • junky • lousy • shoddy • inferior • third rate

Make a list of all the crappy people
and things that remind you of your ex.

urge
noun

1: a strong force or impulse
<I will resist the urge to call my ex at 2 a.m.>

desire • impulse • compulsion • fancy • yearning

Have the
URGE
to call your ex?

Write a list of the most infuriating,
irritating things about your ex.

blunt
adjective

3 a: abrupt in speech or manner
b: being straight to the point
<Let me be blunt: YOU SUCK>

direct • unsubtle • outspoken • honest • candid

Write a BLUNT letter to your ex.
Simply fill in the blanks below.

Dear ....,

You are the most miserable ....

.... I have ever had.

When I think about you, I want to ....

....

I never told you but I hate your ....

.... I wish I could throw

.... at you and

tell you to ....

Why don't you move to ....

for .... years?

Sincerely,

....

revenge
noun

1: an act or instance of retaliating in order to get even
2: an opportunity for getting satisfaction
<I have been plotting revenge since
the day we broke up>

avenging • eye for an eye • get even • vengeance

Revenge is a dish best served cold.

What do you wish you could do to your ex?

van•dal•ize
verb

1: to damage or tarnish
<I will vandalize this journal, instead of
my ex's car>

mar • destroy • deface • trash • wreck • mutilate

F#@K

Vandalize this page with four-letter words.

Ding! Ding!

three-ring cir•cus
noun

2: something wild, confusing, engrossing, or entertaining
<A simple conversation with my ex turns into a three-ring circus>

spectacle • insanity • comedy • performance • absurdity

Welcome to the
❧ THREE-RING CIRCUS. ❧

Describe a fight that practically landed you
and your ex on the Jerry Springer Show.

lousy
adjective

2: miserably poor or inferior
<Thanks for calling the dinner I slaved over lousy>

lame • bad • rotten • disgusting • gross • poor

Did your ex
bag on you for your
LOUSY cooking?

Describe what you'd like
to serve him or her
next time.

Tonight's menu includes …

bliss•ful
adjective

1: a state of complete happiness
<The peace and quiet now that you're gone is blissful>

paradise • joyful • ecstasy • serenity • peaceful

Describe how BLISSFUL
your life is without your ex.

punch
verb

1: to hit, strike, or apply forcefully; to deliver a blow
<I want to punch a clown when I think of my ex>

beat • belt • slug • strike • smash • whack • nail

Make a list of
things you would like to

PUNCH

when you think
about your ex.

(Don't actually punch them.)

black•mail
verb

1: to extort or coerce by threats of public
exposure
<Don't think I won't blackmail my ex with
the photos I have>

badger • force • make demands • shake down • ransom

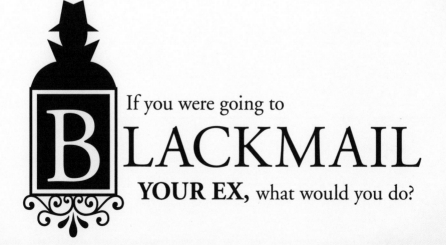

If you were going to **BLACKMAIL YOUR EX,** what would you do?

drop-kick
verb

3: to punt with the top of the foot
<Get out of my way while I drop-kick this journal>

punt • boot • heave • shove • drive • send

Take your frustration out on this journal.

DROP-KICK

this book across the room.

nick•name
noun

1: otherwise known as
<My ex goes by the nickname "Big Fat Jerk">

alias • moniker • nickname • nom de plume • pseudonym

Make a list of the
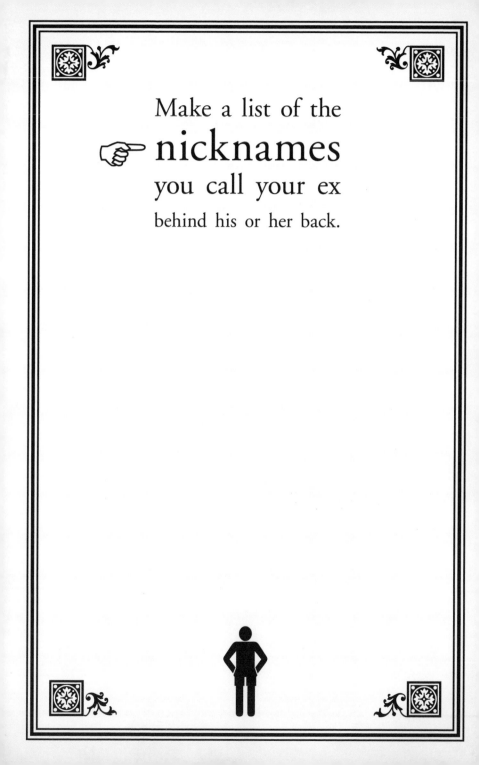 **nicknames**
you call your ex
behind his or her back.

hei•nous
adjective

1 a: morally despicable or abhorrent
4: disgustingly or utterly bad
<Your behavior is heinous>

offensive • horrible • appalling • mean • miserable • vile

Make a list of the most

HEINOUS,

unbelievable things your ex did or said to you.

grate•ful
adjective

1 b: pleasing by reason of comfort supplied or discomfort
alleviated
<I am eternally grateful we broke up>

satisfying • pleasurable • comforting • gratifying • favorable

What are you grateful for?

Make a list of things in your life that don't suck.

(This can help too, maybe.)

hon•est•ly
adjective

1: genuinely
<Honestly, I hate your cat>

really • truly • realistically • justly • candidly

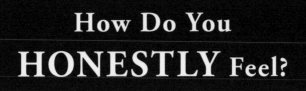

 Remember when you told your ex
how much you liked his or her

.... ?

Tell him or her how
you really feel here.

....

....

....

....

....

....

....

primal scream therapy
noun

1: psychotherapy in which the patient expresses normally repressed anger or frustration especially through spontaneous and unrestrained screams, hysteria, or violence.
<Don't mind my primal scream therapy>

therapeutic • remedy • cure • aid • relief • balm

Primal Scream Therapy

STEP 1:
Open this book wide

STEP 2:
Hold it to your face

STEP 3:
Scream,

"You loser!"

as loud as you can into these pages.

C'mon, you can scream
louder than that!

trash
verb

1: to subject to intense criticism
<I feel better when I trash your
lame new relationship>

rip apart • belittle • bust • assail • tear down

TRASH
THIS PAGE!

Imagine that this voodoo doll is your ex's new boyfriend or girlfriend.

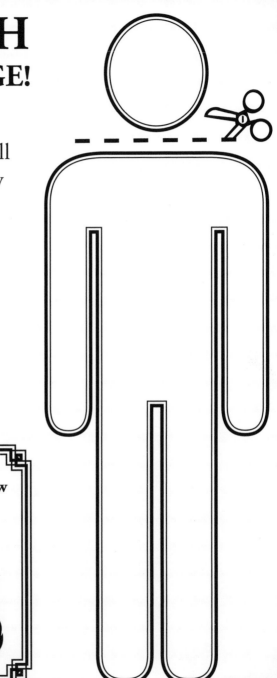

The tools below may help.

de•vour
verb

1: to swallow or eat greedily
<I wish chipmunks would devour my ex>

gobble up • consume • scarf • swallow • engulf • gulp

Choose an animal you wish would

DEVOUR your ex.

choose wisely

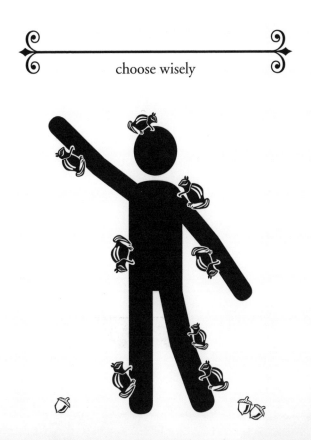

loo•ny
adjective

1: crazy or foolish
<My ex needs to get sent to the loony bin>

cuckoo • daffy • crazy • unstable • flaky • screwy • mad

 **CIRCLE** all the words on this page that describe your ex:

Bitch Jerk **Fat**

LOSER *Princess* Needy

Cheater Stage Five Clinger

LOONY

LAZY **DRAMA QUEEN** **TOOL**

Psycho *Flake*

Wuss

Scrub Evil Liar

MAMA'S BOY Heartbreaker

di•sas•trous
adjective

2: an event marked by lasting distress and
suffering
<That party with my ex turned disastrous
after a few drinks>

calamity • holy mess • misadventure • wreck • ruin

IT WAS DISASTROUS!

Vent about the most hellish event or get-together you had with your ex.

res•cue
verb

1: to free from confinement, danger, or evil
<Someone please rescue me from this
crazy person>

salvage • liberate • free • relieve • get out

RESCUE ME!

What are three things you'd need if
you and your ex were stranded
on a desert island together?

1 ....

2 ....

3 ....

day•dream
verb

1: to have a pleasant visionary or wishful
creation of the imagination
<I like to daydream that you move to Siberia>

muse • imagine • fantasize • pipe dream • stargaze

Daydream about your
happy place where your ex
can't find you.

Describe it here.

bulls•eye

noun

3 a: the center of a target
b: something that precisely attains a desired end
<My aim is excellent when your face is the bullseye>

victory • success • mission accomplished • on the nose

BULLSEYE.

Draw a picture of your ex's face here.

Then tear out this page, hang it on the wall, and throw darts at it.

brain•storm
verb

1: thinking on a question or problem
to produce a sudden bright idea
<I like to brainstorm ways to get this
crazy person out of my life for good>

imagine • conceptualize • ponder • think • mull over

FU brainstorm

Write down the first things about
your ex that come to mind:

Worst quality:

Most annoying trait:

Biggest dealbreaker:

Dumbest lie:

Worst fashion choice:

Grossest habit:

Most overused phrase:

em•bar•rass•ing
adjective

1: a blunder that causes a state of self-consciousness
<My ex falling down drunk at my office holiday
party was embarrassing>

blooper • blunder • flub • gaffe • faux pas • boo boo

You are **embarrassing!**

Describe the most
humiliating thing
your ex ever did.

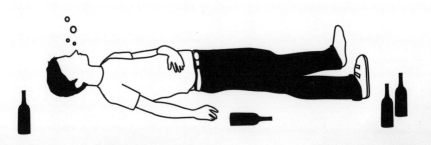

snarky
adjective

1: sarcastic, impertinent, or irreverent in tone or manner
<I hope you will accept my snarky response>

fake • false • guileful • insincere • phony • facetious

IMAGINE YOUR EX WANTS YOU BACK.

What SNARKY thing you would like to say to him or her.

scrib•ble
verb

2: to write or draw hastily or carelessly
3: to cover with worthless writings or drawings
<Your face makes me want to scribble
until this page rips>

claw • scrawl • doodle • scrape • grind • grate • sketch

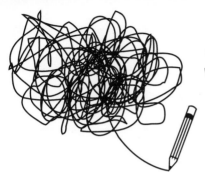

Vent some frustration.

SCRIBBLE

on this page as **hard**
as you can.

drain•ing
adjective

1: to exhaust entirely
2: emptying of all contents
<This relationship is so draining; I'm done>

empty • exhaust • throw in the towel • quit

So DRAINING.

 Write down the number of years this relationship has probably taken off your life.

cel•e•brate
verb

2 a: to honor by refraining from ordinary business
b: to mark by festivities or other deviation from routine
<I plan to celebrate the fact that we are no longer dating>

party • paint the town red • let loose • rejoice • fiesta

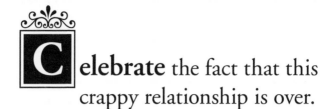

Celebrate the fact that this crappy relationship is over.

Tear this page into tiny pieces of confetti and throw them up in the air.

de•clare
verb

1 a: to make known formally, officially, or explicitly
b: to state emphatically
<Let me declare my true feelings for you>

announce • assert • profess • get off chest • manifest

YOU SUCK !!!!!!!!!!!!

Declare your true feelings for your ex. Open these pages wide and point this book at him or her.

buzz
noun

5: to feel high
<The buzz I get from sniffing this page
helps me forget about my ex>

high • charge • delight • intoxication • free

GET A BUZZ.

Paint this entire
page with a bottle
of White Out or
nail polish.

un•grate•ful
adjective

1: not likely to give or show thanks
<My ex was ungrateful of my attempts
to make things work>

unappreciative • futile • a lost cause • thankless • useless

Your ex was totally **ungrateful.**

Write down all the thoughtful things you
did for your ex that went unappreciated.

LIKE TAKING OUT THE TRASH.

pay•back
noun

2: an act or instance of retaliating
in order to get even
<Making out with your cousin
would be sweet payback>

justice • retribution • vindicate • tit for tat • revenge

OXOXOXOXOXOXOXOXOX xoxoxoxoxoxoxoxox

XOXO   XOXO

XOXO   XOXO

Payback Time!

Name a friend of your ex's you'd make
out with to get back at him or her.

ex•change
verb

1: to recall and swap for another
<I would like to exchange any gifts I ever gave my ex
for a lump of coal>

return • swap • recall • rescind • take back • nix

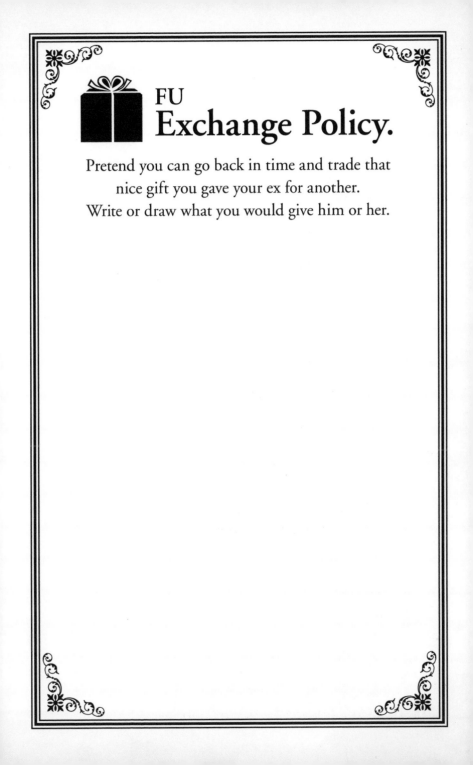

FU
Exchange Policy.

Pretend you can go back in time and trade that
nice gift you gave your ex for another.
Write or draw what you would give him or her.

ran•som
noun

1: a consideration paid or demanded for the release of
someone or something from captivity
<I am holding your cats for ransom>

bribe • pawn • prisoner • token • payoff

I WILL HOLD YOUR DVDs RANSOM

A a a a A B b b C c c D d

d E E e E E F F f G g g H

h h I ï í I I i J J K k K L l

l M m m m N N n o o o O

o P P P P Q q q R r r S S s S

s T t T T u U U u U V v V

W W w X X x Y y y Z Z z

1 2 3 4 5 6 7 8 9 0 0 = + "

" ! @ # $ % ^ & * ? ( ) , .

Cut out letters to make a ransom-style note and leave it for your ex.

fun
noun

1: that which provides amusement or enjoyment
<Our beach vacation was fun;
must have been the cocktails>

jollity • joy • blast • happiness • romp • frolic

Did we ever have **FUN?**

Write about one good time you had with your ex.
C'mon … there's gotta be ONE.

restraining order
noun

1: a legal order issued against an individual to restrict or prohibit access or proximity to another specified individual
<Don't make me get a restraining order against you>

keep back • confine • restrict • harness • control

FU Restraining Order

Write a note to your ex describing why you want him or her to stay **far, far away** from you.

hush-hush
adjective

1: secret; confidential
<I don't have to be hush-hush
now that we're broken up>

classified • dirt • dark secret • under-the-table • illicit

Know a HUSH-HUSH secret about your ex?

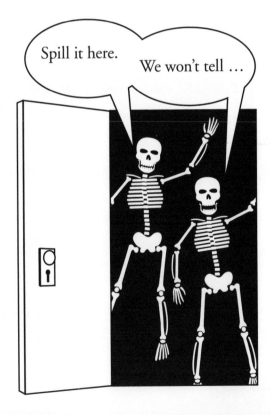

junk
noun

1 a: clutter
b: something of little meaning, worth, or significance
<All our memories are just junk>

odds and ends • garbage • clutter • rubble • scraps

Tear up
old movie tickets,
notes, concert stubs, and other
junk you have leftover from
your ex and tape it to this page.

back off
verb

1: to withdraw from a position
<I'd like to tell my meddling ex to back off>

retreat • resign • yield • wither • submit • fend off

Back Off!

Place your hand on this page with your middle
finger raised and trace; then decorate.

haz•ard
noun

2: a source of great danger
<My ex is a hazard to my sanity>

danger • risk • peril • jeopardy • threat • unsafe

Extreme
Health Hazard

Create a warning
sign for your ex.

DO **NOT** DATE

....
(insert ex's name)

HE/SHE IS

....

....

....

....

dis•trac•tion
noun

1: a means of diversion
<The FU Journal is a welcome distraction
from my problems>

amusement • recreation • preoccupation • relief • repose

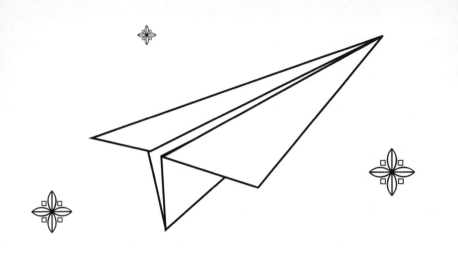

YOU NEED A DISTRACTION.

Tear out this page, and do something
constructive with it (paper airplane, origami, etc).

doomed
adjective

1: the certain failure or destruction of something
<This relationship was doomed from Day One>

hopeless • ill-fated • cursed • kiss of death

This relationship is DOOMED.

Describe the single moment when you
knew this relationship was damned,
like when he wouldn't try sushi.

sin•gle
adjective

1: not married or dating
2: consisting of a separate unique whole
<I am so happy I am single>

independent • unattached • solo • bachelor • free

Make a list of the best things
about being <u>single</u>.

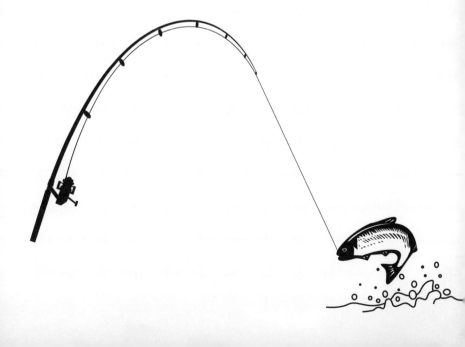

rather
adverb

1: more readily or willingly
<I would rather be watching snails
crawl than hanging out with you>

considerably • noticeably • quite • much • very

I'd **rather** be...

Make a list of activities you would rather do than see your ex's face, like pulling your eyelashes out one by one.

ded•i•cate
verb

1: to set apart to a definite use
<I dedicate "Bye, Bye Love" to my ex>

devote • give over to • appoint • allot • pledge

What song would you like to DEDICATE to your ex?

Title: ....

Lyrics: ....

....

....

....

....

....

....

....

....

....

award
noun

2: something that is conferred or
bestowed especially on the basis of merit
<I present you with the award for
the shadiest significant other>

distinction • honor • prize • badge • accolade • ribbon

Create an AWARD for your ex.

CONGRATULATIONS

_____!

You have won the distinction of

_____

_____

_____

_____

_____

_____

_____

#1
Loser

de•serve
verb

1: worthy of
<You don't deserve to breathe
the same air as I do>

earn • gain • merit • warrant • just desserts

You don't
deserve me

Make a list of all the reasons your ex doesn't deserve you.

chill
adjective

1: marked by or suggestive of utter calm and
unruffled repose or quietude
<After a stiff cocktail, I feel chill>

calm • easygoing • peaceful • placid • relaxed

CHILL
the f#@k out

List things that would help you forget about
your sucky ex, like making out with
an underwear model.

mot•to
noun

1: a sentence, phrase, or word inscribed on something, indicative of its character or use
<The world will appreciate my motto on dating>

slogan • aphorism • byword • epigram • maxim • proverb